I0233981

Resisting Tyranny

Resisting Tyranny

The Story of Matthew Lyon,
Early American Patriot

John Crossley Morgan

Richard Lyon Morgan

RESOURCE *Publications* • Eugene, Oregon

RESISTING TYRANNY
The Story of Matthew Lyon, Early American Patriot

Copyright © 2018 John Crossley Morgan and Richard Lyon
Morgan. All rights reserved. Except for brief quotations in critical
publications or reviews, no part of this book may be reproduced
in any manner without prior written permission from the publisher. Write: Permissions, Wipf and Stock Publishers, 199 W. 8th
Ave., Suite 3, Eugene, OR 97401.

Resource Publications
An Imprint of Wipf and Stock Publishers
199 W. 8th Ave., Suite 3
Eugene, OR 97401

www.wipfandstock.com

PAPERBACK ISBN: 978-1-5326-4465-8
HARDCOVER ISBN: 978-1-5326-4466-5
EBOOK ISBN: 978-1-5326-4467-2

Manufactured in the U.S.A.

To Ruth Lyon, our aunt, who kept family history alive
for us and for generations to come.

We wish to offer words of appreciation
to the following for their help:

Lorraine Brown,
Fair Haven, Vermont Historical Society

Paul Carnahan,
Librarian, Vermont Historical Society

Muir Haman,
Bixby Memorial Library, Vergennes, Vermont

Nancy Staton,
Eddyville, Kentucky

Sally Whittington,
Historical Society, Eddyville, Kentucky

Jack Zeilenga,
Assistant, Curator, Vermont State House

And especially to
Lynda Everman and Don Wendorf,
for their help from the beginning.

Contents

Preface

THERE'S AN IRONY IN writing this book not obvious to the reader. We come from a long line of ministers (and perhaps one pirate), so we paid more attention to that Morgan part of the family tree than other branches. Perhaps it was because our grandfather, G. Campbell Morgan, was a famous preacher who commanded our attention, that we sometimes neglected our other ancestors, the Lyons.

We remember hearing stories of the other side of our family, the Lyons, from our Aunt Ruth who diligently searched the family tree and found our ties to American patriots, including Ethan Allen and Matthew Lyon of the Green Mountain Boys fame in the American Revolution. Neither one of us knew much about Matthew in those days, even though one of us carried the name Lyon as a middle name.

Richard, the historian, started researching Matthew and became interested in his story, especially as Lyon was the first American tried under the 1798 Sedition Act and tossed into a cold and damp Vermont jail, thanks to President John Adams, a person he had criticized for his pomp and arrogance. John, working for the State of Vermont, encountered Lyon in a different way. Walking thorough the Vermont State House, he saw a portrait on the wall that stopped him in his tracks, as he immediately saw a resemblance to his own family. It was a portrait honoring Matthew Lyon hung in the statehouse.

Lyon's life struck us as the story of an American hero, coming to this country from Ireland as an indentured servant, being freed after being traded for two bulls, and rising from these humble beginnings to fight with Ethan Allen's Green Mountain Boys. Later he became an early Vermont Congressman and one of its earliest newspaper publishers, as well as casting the vote that elected Thomas Jefferson as president.

But what really caught our eyes was the fact that he was the first American tried under the 1798 Alien and Sedition Act for openly criticizing then President John Adams. He was fined and thrown into a damp, cold Vermont prison cell in Vergennes. His letters from that jail recalled other letters from jails in later history, martyrs for religious and political liberty—Dietrich Bonhoeffer thrown in prison and later killed in Nazi Germany, and Martin Luther King, Jr., whose letters from a Birmingham, Alabama jail still resonate today.

He was our country's first martyr for freedom of speech as contained in the first amendment to the U.S. Constitution. His rationale for that resistance struck us as important, not just for his times but ours. For this reason, we decided to focus on his resistance to what he considered tyranny then, and what he might say to us today who want to safeguard our liberty.

A word of caution: this is not the full life story of our ancestor. Our intent was to focus on his opposition to tyranny beginning in Ireland and in America leading to his being tried and jailed for speaking out for his right to speak and write even against then President John Adams, and finally to his last years in Kentucky when it was the custom in his time to hold slaves (and he did), how he sought a path to their freedom.

John Crossley Morgan

Richard Lyon Morgan

1. The Life of Matthew Lyon[1]

August 01, 1822

ON THIS DATE, MATTHEW Lyon, one of only a handful of U. S. House Members to represent two states, died. Born in Ireland before sailing to the American colonies in 1765, he entered indentured servitude to pay his passage. In 1774, Lyon moved to the territory that would eventually become Vermont. In 1776, Lyon joined the Continental Army. He was dishonorably discharged following a disputed account in a battle along the northern border, yet Lyon continued as a military scout until he resigned in 1778. Following the Revolution, Lyon helped found the state of Vermont and grew rich from his manufacturing pursuits. He also founded a newspaper supporting Thomas Jefferson's Republican Party in 1793. Following three unsuccessful attempts, Lyon won election to the House of Representatives for the 5th circuit (1797–1799). Lyon remains one of the House's most colorful characters. He participated in an infamous floor brawl with Representative Roger Griswold of Connecticut, and was eventually imprisoned for violating the Sedition Act in 1798, after accusing President John Adams of having "an unbounded thirst for ridiculous pomp." While he railed against the unpopular legislation from his jail cell, Vermont voters re-elected him. When the historic presidential

1. From History, Art & Archives, U. S. House of Representatives, "The Life of Representative Matthew Lyon of Vermont and Kentucky, "http//history. house. gov/Historical Highlight/Detail 36323 and used with permission.

election of 1800 went to the House because of an indeci-sive Electoral College outcome, Lyon cast Vermont's vote for Jefferson. Having not sought re-election in 1800, Lyon moved to Kentucky where he founded several businesses. Lyon won re-election to the House from that state in 1802, becoming the second Member to represent two different states in the House. His opposition to the War of 1812 ended Lyon's congressional career. A downturn in his busi-nesses in 1820 led him to seek a federal patronage position as U. S. negotiator with the Cherokee Indians. It was in this capacity that he died in Spadra Bluff, Arkansas.

2. The Irish Roots of Lyon's Resistance

MOST OF OUR LIFE stories hold the clue to our later lives. This was the same with Matthew Lyon. Except for some memories of one daughter and a later grandson, his early childhood in Ireland remains hidden. He did write an autobiography, but a later descendent says it was stored in an attic and eaten by mice. In a way, perhaps that is fitting for this larger than life person whose story would seem better fitted to film (something we may consider down the road).

However, there are some tentative conclusions that might be drawn from what we do know to put some flesh on the bones of his story, especially as it pertains to his lifelong battle against what he perceived as injustices from elites and those in power.

Lyon was born in Wicklow County, Ireland, probably on July 14, 1749, although some say he was born in 1750. Wicklow was one of the last districts conquered by the British, so there was early on in its history a sense of feeling oppressed by an outside power.

Lyon probably attended school in Dublin where he received a basic education, including the study of Latin. This probably was the extent of his formal education, though he was given training in the trade of printer and bookbinder, which might explain later in America why he sent his son to learn from another printer, Ben Franklin. It might also explain why he set up presses in both Vermont and Kentucky, and used these to promote his ideals and rail against those who sought to take away the rights of people to speak and write without fear.

Of his parents, we know little. We can feel the sadness he must have felt when as a young teenager he said goodbye to his mother while she was sleeping so he could leave for America. There is some reason to believe his father was part of a movement in Ireland called the White Boys, as he probably had been a small farmer whose land was confiscated by the British and who may have been jailed and eventually killed for his resistance. This probably resulted in reducing his family to poverty. Many emigrated to America to seek new lives, Lyon being one.

The beginnings of Matthew Lyon's early life, therefore, bore some resemblances to the situation he found in the new world. He was a member of a class of people oppressed by a stronger outside power, the same empire which ruled the American colonies. And there was resistance in the air, the corruption part of the ruling elite's pattern of behavior. Catholics, for example, most of the Irish population, were excluded from seats or voting in the ruling authority, just as in the beginning, American colonists were taxed without representation.

One early Irishman, Charles Lucas, a printer and advocate for Irish rights, may have served as Lyon's model later. Lucas edited and printed the *Freeman's Journal*, which was democratic in philosophy, hurling invectives at the ruling party. For his outspokenness, Lucas was targeted an enemy of the people and ordered to be arrested. Both Lucas and Lyon admired Ben Franklin. Franklin stayed with Lucas on a visit to Ireland and Lyon sent his son, James, to learn the printing craft from Franklin.

How Lyon escaped and came to America in 1765, the same year as the passage of the stamp act in America, is another incredible chapter of his life. According to his daughter, Elizabeth A. Roe, he ran away from home, stealing away on a ship, the captain promising his safe voyage but later upon arrival indenturing as a servant (some call this "white slavery"), selling him to the highest bidder in New York City who happened to be a Connecticut businessman who took him there, where he needed to work off the price of the voyage. He later was traded to another for a "yoke of bulls," something Lyon would later adopt as a badge of courage while serving in the U. S Congress by swearing his actions were done "by the bulls that redeemed me!"

While the specific details of his early years in Ireland cannot be ascertained, what seems clear are various themes that came to light later in America.

First, after his father died, Lyon's family probably was reduced to poverty and ruled over by an oppressive class that took away their lands, jailed the leaders for resisting, and stifled any oppression. For the rest of his life, he resisted those who exercised power over others unfairly. The ruling elite, whether in Ireland or America, were usually the object of his scorn.

Second, though an indentured servant in Connecticut, Lyon strove to get ahead. He learned business from the two masters under whom he served, and later when settling in Vermont or Kentucky, built town around businesses using the power of rivers to create mills and ironworks to build needed products, whether nails or ships. He was an entrepreneur who made his living through hard work. No wonder, then, he resented those who by inheritance made their way in the world. They were the privileged class to him. He saw himself as someone who took advantage of the opportunities in the new world he might never have had in Ireland.

Finally, he learned the printing trade early in Dublin, and carried this skill with him to the new world. It was his newspapers and magazines in Vermont that gave him a vehicle for protesting what he considered the oppression of the ruling class, one of whom, John Adams, particularly irked him.

For the first years of his ventures in Vermont, Lyon spent most of his time and energies building his businesses while also serving the public good in other ways. The first time he ran for Congress, he lost, but later won and in 1797 took his seat in the new American government. His political philosophy made him part of the new Republican Party, and he was a strong supporter of Thomas Jefferson, casting the vote which made him president. He opposed centralized power and supported state and local forms of governance. He believed in the right to speak and write without fear of repression. He also believed that the basis of the new republic was to empower people to make their own choices and build their lives, and this was to be based on individual initiative not privilege.

3. Defender of Free Speech in 1798

MATTHEW LYON HAD ALREADY gained notoriety through his brawl with Federalist, Roger Griswold, on the floor of Congress. But, Lyon took center stage in his opposition to John Adams and the Alien and Sedition Acts of 1798. A few weeks before leaving Philadelphia on June 20,1798, Lyon had written a letter to the *Spooner's Vermont Journal* as a response to an unsigned letter which had attacked him. In that letter, Lyon criticized the president's "unbounded thirst for ridiculous pomp, foolish adulation and selfish avarice."[1]

In a series of speeches in towns and villages in his district, Lyon waged verbal warfare against the "aristocrats" in Vermont and in Philadelphia. But Lyon's advocacy for free speech became a major issue when Congress passed, and John Adams signed, the Alien and Sedition Acts of 1798. The text of the Alien and Sedition Acts provided that (if) " . . . any persons shall unlawfully combine or conspire together, with intent to oppose any measure or measures of the . . . United States . . . they shall be deemed guilty of a high misdemeanor . . . ." It further prohibited citizens to " . . . write, print, utter, or publish . . . any false, scandalous . . . writing or writings against the government of the United States . . . with intent to defame the said government . . . or to bring them . . . into contempt or disrepute; or to excite against them . . . the hatred of the good people of the United States, or to stir up sedition . . . then such person . . . shall be

1. Wharton, *State Trials*, 33. See Appendix for full text of the Alien and Sedition Acts.

punished by a fine not exceeding two thousand dollars, and by imprisonment not exceeding two years." President John Adams signed the statute into law five days later, on July 15, 1798, the same day as Matthew Lyon's 49th birthday! It was quite apparent that Adams and the Federalists were trying to ram this law into action, and muzzle all attempts of any speech or press that was critical of their policies.

Lyon predicted that he would be the first to be indicted, tried, convicted and imprisoned in violation of the Alien and Sedition Acts, and he was right. But, "Rugged Matt the Democrat," as he was called, could not be silenced. On October 1, five days before his indictment, Lyon published a magazine, called *The Scourge of Aristocracy and Repository of Important Political Truths.* His eldest son, James Lyon, edited the publication whose mission was "to strengthen the cause of Republicanism and truth against Aristocracy and falsehood."

When criticized for writing strong words against the President, Lyon wrote, "I am bound by oath. . . to oppose wrongheaded policies."[2] In no uncertain words, Lyon blamed the Alien and Sedition Acts on President Adams and didn't hesitate to claim that the bill represented a conspiracy of power to silence critics. "Its provisions are a refinement upon Despotism, and present an image of the utmost fearful Tyranny."[3] Lyon warned that under the Alien and Sedition Acts people " . . . had to hold their tongues and make toothpicks out of their pens." But not Matthew Lyon!

The die was cast. On October 3, 1798, a Grand Jury had been called at Rutland, Vermont, fifteen miles from Fairhaven and two days later, on October 5, Lyon would be indicted for sedition. On October 7, he was formally indicted, becoming the first to be accused of violating the

2. *Scourge of Aristocracy.*
3. *Ibid,* October 20. 1798.

Alien and Sedition Acts, and "with malicious intent" to bring the President and government of the United States into contempt." Lyon was accused on three counts: The first pertained to the letter Lyon had written in the *Spooner Vermont Journal* on June 20, 1798. That letter was mailed to the *Journal* three weeks before the Alien and Sedition Acts became law. At his trial, Lyon pointed out that although his letter had been published after the law had been enacted, he had written it before its passage. Ironically, Lyon was being punished for violating a law that did not exist when he wrote the letter.

The other two counts of the indictment pertained to the Joel Barlow letter that Lyon had been quoting publicly all summer long. The offending sections stated that Adams had stolen ideas from Englishman, Edmund Burke, and that President Adams belonged in the madhouse. Though Lyon had not written the letter himself, the Alien and Sedition Acts had made it a crime to "assist" in spreading seditious words.

When the *Aurora,* a paper edited by Benjamin Franklin Bache, and grandson of Ben Franklin, first heard of the Alien and Sedition Acts, it published the text of the law alongside the first amendment. The paper made it clear that the Act not only violated the Constitution, but key virtues of Republicanism. The *Aurora* was launched in October 1790, and was originally called *General Advertiser and Political Commercial, Agricultural and Literary Journal.* The editorial office was on the first floor of 322 Market Street in Philadelphia. The newspaper proclaimed in its first issue, "The Freedom of the Press is the Bulwark of Liberty."[4] The *Aurora* was published six days a week in Philadelphia for thirty years (1794-1824).

4. *Aurora,* June 6, 1798.

Bache was indicted for seditious libel against the president and the executive branch under common law. He appeared in court, posted bail, and received a trial date for the October session. On September 10, Bache died, a victim of the yellow fever epidemic. Although Bache died before the trial, his resistance to Federalism continued from his grave. An article published in the *Boston Chronicle*, two months after his death, told of an imaginary debate between Bache and a prominent Federalist journalist, editor of the *United States Gazette*, John Fenno. Bache says, "(Do) you think that persecution was likely to stop the thoughts and pen of a free American?"[5]

One integral aspect of the Alien and Sedition Acts was its assault on freedom of the press. The law prohibited newspaper criticism of the President. This was true even though the Bill of Rights, with its guarantee of press freedom was already seven years old in 1798. The Federalists secured fourteen indictments under the Alien and Sedition Acts, targeting all the most prominent Republican editors. Through their coverage of the Acts, printers not only reported on public affairs but participated in politics themselves. They even labeled themselves as martyrs to the cause of liberty. Indeed, freedom of the press was a bright light in the darkness of tyranny.

Lyon Arrested, Tried, and Convicted

October 5, a deputy marshal knocked on the door of Lyon's home in Fairhaven and served him with an arrest warrant. Lyon posted bail, until his appearance at trial the following Monday in Rutland. Lyon decided to have a speedy trial. Bad weather caused the delay of his lawyers, so Lyon

5. *Boston Chronicle.*

decided to represent himself. The presiding judge was to be Supreme Court Associate Justice William Paterson, an avid Federalist and friend and sometime dinner companion of President Adams. The federal district attorney, Charles Marsh, would prosecute the case. Marsh, a Federalist, was a member of the U. S. House of Representatives from Vermont. It would seem that Marsh was simply play acting a role in the drama, with its denouement already decided. Even the twelve jurors were handpicked by the Federalists. Apparently, the trial was rigged against Lyon before it began, a miscarriage of justice.

On October 7, the trial began, and 12 jurors were chosen. Both sides challenged some jurors. Lyon's first motion was to dismiss the case because the Alien and Sedition Acts were unconstitutional. Paterson said that the validity of the Acts could not be disputed, but Lyon's letters were the real issue, whether they were seditious. The trial only lasted one day. Paterson's charge to the jury was that if Lyon had published the letters and they were contemptible of the President and the government, they must bring a verdict of guilty. After deliberating for one hour, eleven of the twelve jurors were prepared to find Lyon guilty immediately. A twelfth held out for a while and finally relented, so by 8 p. m. , a guilty verdict was brought against Lyon.

The next morning Judge Paterson admonished Lyon for not recognizing "the mischiefs which flow from an unlicensed abuse of government." Paterson then slapped him with a fine of $1,000 and four months in prison. It was obvious that Paterson wanted to make an example of Lyon. In Connecticut, the *Connecticut* Courant praised Lyon's sentence and pending imprisonment with a couplet:

Matthew Lyon, peeping through his grate,
The fetter'd Delegate of Vermont state.[6]

Lyon was then placed in the hands of Jabez Fitch, a district marshal and avowed enemy of Lyon. From the moment, the sentence was handed down Fitch treated Lyon like an incorrigible criminal, not like a US congressman. Adding insult to injury, Finch did not take Lyon to a prison near Lyon's home in Rutland but deliberately took him forty-five miles to the north, to Vergennes, a Federalist stronghold, in western Vermont. Although innocent of any crime, Lyon was paraded like a circus freak through many villages, loyal to Adams and the Federalists. One can imagine the jeers and catcalls this champion of liberty must have endured throughout the long journey, let alone the indignities and inconveniences thrust upon him by his captors. Lyon rode in front, with two armed deputies waiting for Lyon to run or resist. But like a lamb led to the slaughter, Lyon rode meekly and quietly amid the howling jeers of the crowd who watched him pass their way. On the journey, Lyon asked for pen and paper, but Jabez Fitch refused his request.

On October 10, the journey ended at Vergennes, and Fitch led him to a cell on Main Street. The prison had empty cells, but Fitch locked him in a common cell where he would have to share quarters with "horse-thieves, money-makers, run away negroes or any kind of felons."[7] The cell was just twelve feet long and sixteen feet wide, Lyon reported, with a "necessary in one corner, which affords a stench about equal to a Philadelphia docks in the month of August."[8] The cell had no heat, and Lyon stayed warm by wearing a coat and marching back and forth in the cramped

6. *Connecticut* November 28, 1798.

7. Wharton, *State Trials.*

8. Ibid.

cell. Lyon described his trial and prison existence in a letter he wrote from prison to Stevens Thomson Mason, which will be discussed in the next chapter. This horrible existence Lyon had to endure, would destroy a person's spirit. But not this advocate of freedom. For these fourth months Matthew Lyon lived the words of Nietzsche, "That which doesn't kill me makes me stronger." Like the proverbial Phoenix, this "Lion of the House" would rise from the ashes of this unfair imprisonment to fight for freedom yet another day. The Alien and Sedition Acts of 1798 may have been the first great test of whether the United States would live out its claim to be the bulwark of liberty for all.

4. Words from Prison: Letter to His Supporters

IMAGINE YOU ARE SITTING in a cramped prison cell in Vergennes, Vermont, on the morning of October 9, 1798. The cell is 16 ft. long and 12 ft. wide and is crowded with all manner of felons and hardened criminals. There is a "necessary" in one corner, which causes " . . . a stench about equal to the Philadelphia docks in the month of August." It is bitter cold, with no heat from a fireplace, and you pace back and forth on the frozen dirt floor of your cell with your heavy coat drawn tightly around your body. There is a half-moon hole through the door, through which your friends can look through and speak to you. The only light comes from a window crossed by nine iron bars. You look through the ever-open window and you can see the Otter River, frozen so deep that it formed ice that glistened in the sunlight of that clear, cold, Fall day. You are a writer, and request paper and pen, but that is denied. You have been sentenced by a judge who detests you after a mock trial with a jury more intent on conviction than justice. If you can picture yourself in this scene, you can identify with the congressman, Matthew Lyon, to whom this happened.

It would have been easy for Lyon to be bitter and resentful at this injustice, and being dispatched from his home in Fairhaven to these deplorable conditions. On the contrary, much to the shock of his enemies, the fiery Lyon became meek and mild, a model prisoner. He obeyed all the rules, somehow got along with his fellow prisoners and refused to react to the indignities of prison. Lyon had known what it was like to be an indentured servant, and realized that his prison term could be used to his political advantage. After a few weeks, his request for paper and pen was granted, and he wrote letters published in *The Scourge of Aristocracy* and later printed in the *Aurora*. The caged Lion would still roar!

Lyon records the details of his imprisonment in a letter to Senator Steven Thompson Mason. It was ironic that Matthew Lyon was jailed in Vergennes. Ethan Allen, Lyon's relative by marriage, was among those who incorporated the town in 1788. Allen named it after Comte de Vergennes, a French statesman who sided with the American cause for independence.

Lyon did have a moment of sadness when he learned that his friend and colleague, Benjamin Franklin Bache, died on September 10th a victim of the yellow fever epidemic. Bache and Lyon were close allies in fighting tyranny and standing for the freedom of the press. He wrote from prison, "I mourn with you the death of our good friend, Bache. He was too good a man to be tortured with the Sedition law—God saw him in that light and took him to himself."

When Lyon's old cronies, the Militia of the Green Mountain Boys of Vermont, heard of Lyon's imprisonment, they were furious and plotted to free him from the jail. Lyon had fought alongside Ethan Allen (to whom he was related through his first marriage to Mary Horsford) in the capture of the British Fort Ticonderoga. The Militia was ready to storm the prison at Vergennes, tear it down, and set Lyon free. When a large company of his followers appeared at the prison, Lyon addressed them and urged them not to resort to violence. Instead, he urged them to correct abuse at the voting polls. Lyon's peaceful non-resistance to this threat seems a precursor of the non-violent resistance advocated later by Mahatma Gandhi and Martin Luther King, Jr., both also unjustly put in prison. Lyon was content to ride out his four-month prison sentence without resorting to violence. Although the roaring voice of the "Lyon of the House" seemed silenced, he began to speak through letters from his prison cell. He wrote a classic letter to his friend, Senator Steven Thomson Mason of Virginia. The date line included the words " In Jail at Vergennes."[1] This letter was widely circulated throughout the country by the *Democratic Press*, and became a clarion call for liberty for all.

Lyon minced no words in his criticism of President John Adams. He first stated that the charge that he "having maliciously & with intent" written at Philadelphia, a letter dated the 20th of June, and printed the same at Windsor in the newspaper, *The Vermont Journal*, was not true. He was simply printing the truth about the Adams Administration.

As to the President, John Adams, Lyon wrote these scathing words: "As to the Executive, when I shall see the efforts of that power bent on the promotion of the comfort, happiness, and accommodation of the people, that Executive shall have my zealous and uniform support, but when I shall see, on the part of the Executive,every consideration of the public welfare swallowed up in a continuous grasp for power, in an unbounded thirst for ridiculous pomp, foolish adulation, and selfish avarice; when I shall behold men of real merit turned out of office, for no other reason but independency of sentiment, when I see men of firmness, merit, years, abilities and experience discarded in their applications for office, for fear they possess that independence and men of meanness preferred for their ease with which they take up and advocate opinions, the consequences of which

1. James McLaughlin, *Matthew Lyon: The Hampden of Congress,* 342-355.

they know little—when I see the sacred name of religion employed as a state engine to make mankind hate and persecute one another, I shall not be their humble advocate."[2]

Lyon ended his letter to Mason with these words, "I who have been a football for dame fortune all my life I am best able to bear it." He refused to accept that the President was infallible, and believed Adams had made him the subject of a witch hunt. Lyon had become a martyr for freedom.

Lyon commented on the Vermont Congressional Election, in which he had failed by a single ballot to be reelected. Lyon had outrun his closest rival, Stanley Williams, by 3,442 votes to 1,554. But since Lyon had not gained a majority of the votes, a runoff was scheduled for December while Lyon was still in jail. *For the first time in American history, a candidate for Congress conducted his campaign from a federal prison.* Lyon had to campaign for re-election from a prison cell. Being denied the freedom to make campaign speeches proved providential, as Lyon's followers waged an incessant campaign for Lyon in his congressional district of western Vermont. Their efforts were rewarded when almost two thousand more voters turned out than in September. Lyon won an overwhelming victory, beating his nearest competitor, Williams by a vote of 4,776 to 2,444. *Lyon had become the first congressman In the United States to be elected while in prison.*

Several thousand Vermonters signed a petition, asking the President to pardon Lyon, and release him from prison. The Reverend John Cosens Ogden, rector of St. John's Episcopal Church in Portsmouth, New Hampshire, and a friend of Lyon, led the delegation. Ogden had worked closely with Lyon in Episcopal conventions according to historian Aleine Austin. After traveling four hundred miles to Philadelphia, they presented their petition to the President. Adams

2. Ibid.

asked if Lyon was behind the petition. When told he was not, Adams denied the petition on the basis that "penitence precedes pardon."

For his role in supporting Lyon, Ogden became a marked man. On his return to Vermont, he visited his old hometown of Litchfield, Connecticut, and promptly was arrested and thrown into jail. Ogden served four months. The *Connecticut Courier* dubbed him "Rev. Gaolbird."

After learning of his re-election, Lyon wrote a letter from his prison cell in Vergennes to the freemen of his district. He dated it January 12, 1799.[3] Lyon called his re-election a blow to the Alien and Sedition Acts and thanked them for doing what a stacked jury could not do, that he was not guilty of "pretended crimes." In no uncertain words, Lyon retold his story he had written in an earlier letter with these words, "The story has already been told in every country where representative government is known, that one of the national representatives of the United States of America, has been imprisoned for writing and publishing that when the executives are doing right they shall have his support, but ever they do wrong, he would not be their advocate."

At eight o'clock on the morning of February 9, 1789, Lyon was released from jail. Before he left the jail, he stopped and said, "I am on my way to Philadelphia." This was not a statement of his itinerary. He had heard that his old nemesis, Fitch, had summoned lawyers to read his letters from jail. The Federalists hoped to find more evidence, and if they did, would re-arrest him. But Lyon outsmarted them. He knew that congressmen, en route to Congress, could not be arrested (Article I, Section 6). Lyon made the

---

3. *Vermont Gazette,* January 1799.

announcement that he was going to congress in Philadelphia to prevent any attempt by the Federalists to re-arrest him.

A huge crowd welcomed him, as he stepped from the jail. Boarding a coach drawn by four horses, with the American flag at its head, Lyon accompanied by his wife, Beulah, made a triumphant journey to Philadelphia. The crowd that had assembled at the jail to celebrate his freedom followed his coach for twelve miles to Middlebury, with rousing cheers. Even school children paraded for him and cheered their brave congressman as a victor over tyranny. Never had western Vermont seen such a jubilant parade. Then the procession stopped at the States Arms Tavern in Bennington, Vermont, where Lyon's friend, Anthony Haswell, delivered the welcoming speech. Haswell, like Lyon, an immigrant and printer, published the *Vermont Gazette*. In 1785, Haswell had championed Lyon's cause and called his trial "persecution not prosecution." Earlier, Haswell had infuriated the religious establishment (Congregationalism) by publishing Ethan Allen's *Reason: The Only Oracle of Man*. Lyon was related to Allen and spent much time with Allen in Vermont. There is little doubt that Lyon read and embraced some of Allen's philosophy of Deism.

In his address to the assembled crowd, Haswell congratulated Lyon on his freedom and praised the Constitution as "the glory of the land" and "the cement of the union." He also stressed the importance of the Bill of Rights. Haswell even wrote a song for the celebration. The last stanza went like this:

> *Come take a glass and drink his health*
> *Who is a friend of Lyon.*
> *First martyr under federal law,*
> *The junto tried to try it on.*[4]

4. Quoted in James Morton Smith, *Freedom Fetters. 245.*

Nine months later, Haswell suffered the same fate as Lyon. He was tried and convicted of "The publication of seditious statements in the advertisement of Lyon's lottery."The fact was all that Haswell had done was to publish an advertisement by two subscribers to the fund-raising money to pay Lyon's fine. But, Haswell was convicted of violating the Alien and Sedition Acts and was imprisoned on May 9, 1800, first at Rutland, and later in the jail at his home town of Bennington. Since, unlike Lyon in the Vergennes jail, Haswell had easy access to friends and wrote many communiques, his imprisonment was not as harsh as Lyon had endured. When he was released on July 9, 1800, friends postponed the July 4th celebration for five days, so that Haswell's freedom could be aligned with Independence Day. As the prison doors opened, cannons roared, the crowd cheered, and the band struck up "Yankee Doodle."

*What a transformation had occurred in those four months since Lyon's imprisonment!*Hauled off to jail as a convicted felon, guilty of a crime he did not commit, Lyon was returning to Congress as a political martyr who had won over tyranny.

Lyon was often toasted with these words:

> *Colonel Matthew Lyon, The Martyr to the Cause of Liberty and the Rights of Man: Long may his suffering bring good out of evil, by arousing the people to guard their rights and oppose every unconstitutional measure.*[5]

On Wednesday, October 20, the Annals of Congress simply stated, "Matthew Lyon, from Vermont, appeared and took his seat in the House."[6]A simple record of fact, but

5. Smith, 246.

6. Wharton, 341.

those words spoke volumes about Matthew Lyon's victory over tyranny.

In 2006, then Representative Bernie Sanders, now Senator from Vermont, spoke to the House of Representatives, introducing a bill that would name the post office in Fair Haven, Vermont, in honor of Matthew Lyon. In that speech, Sanders said,

"At a time when we find ourselves struggling to balance the security of our country with the liberties we cherish, I can think of no better time to honor one of our nation's champions of the First Amendment's right of free speech."[7]

---

7. Bernie Sanders, *Speech in House of Representatives,* April 27, 2006.

5. Last Letter to John Adams

THE ROOTS OF MATTHEW Lyon's resistance to tyranny and his opposition to President John Adams can better be understood in the light of his Irish roots before he came to America. There were two dominant themes in Matthew Lyon's early life that help understand his later life in America. The first was that he experienced poverty and exploitation at the hands of a ruling power, the British Parliament imposing itself on the wool trade in his native Ireland. While the historical records are not always clear, there is some reason to believe Lyon's father resisted the British and was hanged for advocating for the rights of farmers. The second experience was his coming to America as an immigrant in 1765. His resistance to tyranny in America, in a country in which freedom was lauded for all people, not just the elite, was deeply rooted in his early years in Ireland as a young boy with little money, no hopes of a job, and no family awaiting him. He was an indentured servant who paid for his passage by having to work off the amount due to someone who employed him.

Lyon's resistance to tyranny in any form came from these experiences as a child in Ireland where he saw his family and neighbors suffering under the yoke of the British and the oppression of the poor and working class by those in power. His was a lifetime of seeking opportunity for himself and others in the face of oppression by the wealthy. No wonder the magazine he and his son founded and edited was called *The Scourge of Aristocracy and Repository of Important Political Truths.*

His later experiences as a legislator and newspaper publisher reinforced his early experiences of mistrust of any governmental power which sought to silence dissent or free speech. Thus, when the U. S. Congress approved the Alien and Sedition Acts of 1798, Lyon was especially incensed, believing not only were they against the first amendment of the Constitution approved by the same Congress seven years earlier, but specifically directed toward him as a critic of the president. Lyon believed Adams was using him as an example to stifle free speech. (To read the pertinent section of the Alien and Sedition Acts under which Lyon was tried, convicted and jailed, look in the Appendix).

Lyon's Revenge in 1800

Matthew Lyon got sweet revenge in the tumultuous, crisis-ridden election of 1800. Lyon had vigorously campaigned for Thomas Jefferson in Virginia. In the election, Jefferson won the popular vote over Adams and Pinckney by 61. 3 percent to 18. 7 per cent. Yet, due to the electoral system, Jefferson and Aaron Burr ended with 73 electoral votes apiece. Adams won 65 electoral voters. The Constitution provides that, in case of a tie or if no candidate received the majority of the Electoral College, that the House of Representatives, voting by state, must choose a president from the top two candidates. Each of the sixteen states had a single vote, with nine needed to elect the next president. The balloting dragged on through thirty-five ballots. On that ballot, Vermont cast a blank vote, since its votes were divided between Lewis Morris, a Federalist, and Matthew Lyon.

Finally, on February 17, 1801 on the thirty-sixth ballot, Lewis Morris the Federalist, withdrew. Now as the sole representative from Vermont, Lyon cast the deciding vote that elected Thomas Jefferson as the third President of the United States, who ended up with ten states to four for Burr. One could almost feel the despair of the Federalists and jubilation of the Democratic Republicans that historic moment.

The Letter to John Adams

Here are some key parts of Lyon's letter:

City of Washington,

59 minutes before one, a. m. , March 4, 1801

Fellow Citizen:

Four years ago this day, you became President of the United States, and I a Representative of the people in Congress; this day has brought us once more on a level; the acquaintance we have had together entitles me to the liberty I take, when you are going to depart for Quincy, by and with the consent and advice of the good people of the United States, to bid you a hearty farewell. This appears to me more proper, as I am going to retire, of my own accord, to the extreme western parts of the United States, where I had fixed myself an asylum from the persecutions of a party, the most base, cruel, assuming and faithless, that ever disgraced the councils of any nation. That party are now happily humbled in "dust and ashes, before the indignant frowns of an injured country," but their deeds never can be forgotten . . . . I beg you to reflect. . . on your childish nonsense about dividing the people from the government. . . .

I hope, sir, you are not past blushing at what a school boy would be ashamed of. The people of this country can never be divided from the government; you have brought yourself into hatred and contempt with them; but they never could be induced to view you and your executive officers as the government. No! The government they love and respect, and have accordingly put it into better hands. You now have leisure, sir, to look over your second speech to the same Congress, when I hope you will recollect how you swelled and strutted when you were abusing the nation you were hypocritically pretending to make up differences with.

Look at the list of laws which you sanctioned. . . giving new and unconstitutional powers to yourself. . . . I will not pretend to describe sensations they will produce, when you reflect how they buoyed up your pride, flattered your vanity, and persuaded you the day was approaching and nigh at hand, when an hereditary crown would be offered to you . . . .

You came to the administration, sir, under the most favorable auspices at the time when there were parties in this country, they were by no means hostile to each other; when the increasing revenue was sinking the public debt; when the Federal judiciary held a state of popularity in this country, and were regarded with respect; when the contributions toward the public expense sat tolerably easy on the people, when this country was considered as an asylum for the oppressed of all nations, and there was a great influx of foreign riches, industry and ingenuity; when this country was happy in the freedom of speech and of the press; when the Constitution was considered a barrier against legislative, executive and judicial encroachments. And before the people were divided into castes of gentlemen and simple men; before offices, places and contracts, were considered as the exclusive rights of the favorite caste. Reflect a little, sir, and see this awful change made in four short years. . . . You commenced your career, sir, by professions; your mad zeal for monarchy and Britain; your love of pomp, your unhappy selection of favorites, your regardlessness of the public treasure, the hard earnings of your fellow citizens, has divided the people into parties and fostered among them envy, malice and rancorous hatred towards each other, father has been set against son, and son against father, brother against brother, neighbors and friends have lost their former relish for the social enjoyments. . . .

Under your administration, sir, a system of appointments has been established by which implicit faith in your infallibility and a knack of discoloring the truth became the only qualification to office . . . .

The judiciary, sire, under your untoward administration, have made alarming encroachments on the rights of man . . . .

Under your administration, sir, and with your consent, your fellow-citizens have had a heavy addition to the tax on salt their houses and lands have been subjected to an unprecented tax . . . .

An alien law bears your signature, which unconstitutionally subjected to your sovereign will the liberty and banishment of every alien . . . . the best and the most able and useful emigrants have been deterred from coming to this country, and many have been obliged to fly from your vindictive wrath . . .

Perhaps in no other instance has our Constitution, our sacred bill of rights, have been more shamefully, more barefacedly trampled on, than in the case of the passage of the bill called the Sedition Act. This, sir, was your darling hobby horse.

By this law, you expected to have all your follies, your absurdities, and your atrocities buried in oblivion. You thought by its terrors to shut the mouths of all but sycophants and flatterers, and to secure yourself in the Presidency at least; but how happily have you been disappointed, —the truth has issued from many a patriot pen and press, —and you have fallen, never, never to rise again.

It has availed you little, sir, to have me fined $1,000, and imprisoned four months, for declaring truth long before the Sedition Act was passed. . . . Attempts to stifle an investigation of your conduct only accelerated your fall. . . .

You seem now more than ever bent on mischief. Your vindictive spirit prompts you to do everything in your power to give the succeeding administration trouble; but you are as unfortunate in this as in most of your calculations. Your creatures are generally pliant seeds; they will bend to and fawn upon anybody that is in power. It was power they worshipped in you, not John Adams.

Come, pray sir, cool yourself a little. Do not coil round like the rattlesnake, and bite yourself. No, betake yourself to fasting and prayer awhile. It may be good for both body and soul. . . .

Suffer me to recommend to you that patience and resignation which is characteristic of the holy religion you profess. I hope and pray that your fate may be a warning to all usurpers and tyrants, and that you may, before you leave this world, become a true and sincere penitent, and be forgiven all your manifold sins in the next. I repeat it, this is the sincere wish and prayer of your fellow-citizen.

M. Lyon

6. Lyon's Later Years and Resistance to Slavery

WHILE CAMPAIGNING FOR THOMAS Jefferson in 1799, Lyon visited his friend, Andrew Jackson in Tennessee. Lyon was deeply impressed by the land in the south, and later wrote to Jackson, "Your country is far superior to any I have ever seen, and never has been out of my thoughts since I saw it. To enjoy the blessings of such a country, such soil, and such a climate in a good neighborhood, is what is wished for by your Devoted friend."[1] Once again Lyon was the pioneer, willing to leave friends and enterprises in Fair Haven to journey to a new place, where he had to begin again. Such was the character of Matthew Lyon, a man always driven, restless, and seeking new adventures.

Lyon purchased nearly six thousand acres in Kentucky, and began preparations to close out his life in Fair Haven. He made this daring venture in two stages. An advance party, consisting of his son, James Lyon, Ann, Lyon's 's oldest daughter and her husband John Messenger, his second oldest daughter, Pamelia and her husband, Dr. George Catlett, and his youngest daughter, Lorraine, would be the nucleus of the first settlers. They were joined by ten families from Fair Haven. In 1799, they journeyed to Kentucky, to lay the groundwork for Lyon's future settlement on the Cumberland River. Their task was to clear the land, plant crops, and build houses, in preparation for Lyon's later arrival.

1. Letter from Lyon to Andrew Jackson, February 28, 1800. Quoted in Austin, 171.

Lyon returned to Congress for the 1799-1800 session. Then he returned to New Haven, burned his bridges behind him, and sold his many industries and businesses. He then hurried back to Congress for the turbulent session which finally elected Thomas Jefferson on the 36th ballot.

Matthew Lyon, his second wife, Beulah, their young children and ten other families, including several artisans. One can visualize the long line of white covered wagons, as they left Fair Haven. The journey of 400 miles took them over mountains in Pennsylvania to Pittsburgh, where they spent the winter. There they prepared for their journey down the Ohio River. Mechanics used the winter months building flat boats and creating a fleet of boats. That spring they began the journey down the Ohio River to Eddyville, Kentucky.

Their arrival at Eddyville on July, 1891, was a mixture of celebration and grief. They celebrated their arrival, but heard the sad news that Lyons' beloved 17-year- old daughter, Lorraine, had become sick upon her arrival in Eddyville, and died of "bilious fever."Biographer, J. Fairfax McLaughlin, relates the way Lyon heard of his daughter's death. "Colonel Lyon and his wife, who when they landed, were taken aside by Dr. Caldwell, and in as gentle manner as he could employ, broke the news to them.[2]There was irony in her sad death. Matthew Lyon had named his daughter, Lorraine, grandniece of Ethan Allen, because of his friendship with Ethan Allen. Allen's daughter, Lorraine, died in 1783, at the age of 20. After visiting the grave of Lorraine Lyon, (the first person to be buried in the River View Cemetery in Eddyville), Lyon was overcome with grief. Lyon County historian, Odell Walker, write, "Of all of the upheavals, stormy and turbulent life of Matthew Lyon, one

2. J. Fairfax McLaughlin, *Matthew Lyon; The Hampden of Congress: ABiography.* Forgotten Books, 2012.

event seemed to stand out as the most devastating, crush-
ing, and sad happenings of his entire life (when) he received
the heartbreaking news that his lovely daughter, Lorraine
had died."[3] In time, Matthew Lyon moved himself into all
the business enterprises in his new town. This seemed to
assuage his grief. In Eddyville, Lyon used his knowledge
and skill to carve out an empire in Eddyville, as he had in
Fair Haven. His new business complex included a saw mill,
a paper mill, iron furnace, tannery, wagon shop, and retail
store.

Among Lyon's many business activities in his new sur-
roundings was bookselling. This venture formed the basis
for Lyon's business relationship with Matthew Carey, an
Irish born Republican bookdealer and economist. Carey
had worked in Ben Franklin's printing office. Lyon described his barge as a "moving bookstore." In this way, Lyon
continued his love of publishing which he had done wo well
in Fair Haven.

In no time, with his businesses flourishing, Lyon re-
entered the world of politics. Elected to Congress, he served
the state of Kentucky from 1803-1811. During his tenure in
Congress, Matthew Lyon became the recognized leader of
the Jefferson party in Congress, until he retired from Congress on March 3, 1811,

Lyon's Approach to Slavery

At Eddyville, Lyon had to confront the slavery issue. Vermont was an anti-slavery state. On his farm and household
white labor was not available, since most of the inhabitants
were poor and lived in log cabins. Lyon had been one of
the congressmen who opposed slavery although most of

3. Odell Walker. *Profiles of the Past.* 1994.

the other congressmen owned slaves.[4] George Washington owned 317 slaves, who made possible his whole manner of life. Thomas Jefferson owned over 600 slaves, who were not freed until after his death to pay his enormous debts. Jefferson's approach was both enigmatic and hypocritical. On the one hand, he had drafted a clause in the Declaration of Independence which proclaimed freedom for all, but as a concession to the southern states of South Carolina, and Georgia, it was deleted. The Founders preferred unity and independence and so shoved the slavery issue on the shelf, to be decided at a later time. Jefferson thought slavery was "an extreme depravity unremitting despotism by the owners, and degrading submission for the slaves." Yet because of the many needs of his plantation at Monticello, he never gave his slaves their freedom.

Lyon's contemporaries, James Madison and James Monroe owned slaves. Even Andrew Jackson, who fought for America's freedom against the British, owned slaves. John Adams, Alexander Hamilton, and Thomas Paine were not slave owners.

Lyon was different. He demonstrated his opposition to slavery on the floor of Congress.

The Society of Quakers presented a Memorial to Congress protesting the "oppressed state of our brethren of the African race." The Quakers called on Congress to act against the re-enslavement of 135 North Carolina former slaves the Quakers had freed. Southern Federalists immediately protested the Memorial.

Matthew Lyon, rose in defense of the Quakers. Lyon said, "There was a grievance complained of which certainly ought to be remedied, viz. that a number of black persons who had been set at liberty, were now held in slavery,

4. See Stephen Ambrose, *Founding Fathers and Slave Owners.* Sojourners 2002.

contrary to their right."[5] In siding with the Quakers, Lyon showed that slavery was morally wrong.

So it was that Lyon, needing labor for his household, farm and business enterprises, developed an approach which opposed the tyranny of slave owners. *He treated his slaves as indentured servants which he himself once was.* Mindful of how he had earned his freedom as a young man in Connecticut, he afforded his slaves the same possibility. Furthermore, as one reads the accounts of his relationship to his slaves, they were more persons than property.

The first slave whom Lyon treated as an indentured servant was Chloe. She had fled from a harsh, brutal slave owner and came to Matthew Lyon for sanctuary. Lyon treated her with great kindness and provided a house for her. Mrs. Lyon even made sure she ate the same food as did the Lyons, and wore clothes like the Lyon family and gave her visitation rights to see her slave friends. On one occasion Chloe found a slave, named Anna, hiding in cave to escape her cruel owner. Chloe brought her to Lyon, and agreed that she would be an indentured servant, and work off her purchase price. Anna wanted to marry another slave, George, whom Lyon bought for $1,000. He had George trained as a carpenter for his boat yard, and allowed George to earn his freedom as his indentured servant. Later, Matthew Lyon officiated at the wedding of George and Chloe, and even opened his home to a wedding party that was attended both by the slaves and Lyon family. Lyon's benevolence for the freed slaves went beyond allowing them to earn his freedom. He would give them provisions to move to the free states of Illinois or Ohio. Word soon got around the slaves about the Lyon family's kindness to slaves. Many

---

5. Alein Austin, *Matthew Lyon: New Man of the Democratic Revolution, 1749-1822.*

fled their slave master, and fell on their knees, begging Lyon to buy them.

Religious Significance of the Indentured Servant, Richard

Matthew Lyon never joined a church as far as any records indicate, but had some relationship to the Episcopal Church. Anne Roe, his youngest daughter, claimed Matthew Lyon was a Deist. "My father,' she wrote was a man at that time the world called a kind-hearted, generous, noble minded deist. He believed in an all-wise Creator and preserver of the universe."[6]

The story of the slave, Richard whose religious faith, Lyon allowed is of deeper meaning. The young black man was born in 1774 in North Carolina. His owner taught Richard to read the Bible. Richard experienced a conversion and taught the Gospel to his fellow slaves. Irritated by His preacher, his owner sold him to a Mr. Michelson in Eddyville, who later told him to Matthew Lyon.

Lyon gave Richard half day off on Saturday to visit his family, who were still slaves. On Sundays services were conducted on the back porch of Aunt Chloe's kitchen—an old cabin set some distance from the main house because of fear of fire. Richard held religious services, as both blacks and whites sat on benches made by George and Richard, both indentured servants. Lyon County historian, Odell Walker writes, "the earliest preaching (1808) in Eddyville was the summer kitchen of Matthew Lyon, located on the hill above the Big Spring.[7] The first Methodist Church was

6. Ann Elizabeth Roe. *Aunt Leanna* or *Early Scenes in Kentucky.* , Published in House 1885.

7. Odell Walker, *In Lyon County Saturday Night was Town Day.* Lyon County Historical Society, 2002, 275.

built with a black man as preacher as the preacher, and both whites and blacks as worshippers. This remarkable story was narrated by Elizabeth Lyon Roe in her book *Reflections of Frontier Life.*[8]

The rest of Richard's story has a happy ending. After Richard paid off his debt, Lyon gave him free papers and had it recorded in the courthouse. He also gave him 40 dollars, a workable horse, and subscription to solicit money to buy the freedom of his family of a wife, a boy and a girl. After he had raised the money, Richard and his family left Eddyville and settled Silver Creek in Illinois, a free state. Richard continued his life helping others, and was an active minister of the Gospel and assisting needy immigrants.

Lyon's Final Years

The final two years of Lyon's life were marked by financial disaster and yet a journey to another place. In 1812, Lyon tried to help his friend, Andrew Jackson, in his battle against the British in New Orleans. At his own expense, Lyon built a fleet of flatboats and gun boats.

But, a storm on the Mississippi River sank all but boat and the cargo were lost. Lyon found himself in financial ruin. He became as poor as he was when he came to America in 1749. However, his sons led by Chittenden Lyon, came to his rescue and paid off a debt of nearly $28,000.

Later that year, President James Monroe, a friend of Lyon, appointed him the United States Factor (agent) to the Cherokee Indians in the Arkansas Territory. Lyon settled at Spadra Buff, where he lived out the final two years of his life. After a journey to New Orleans, Lyon visited the town of Eddyville, and soon thereafter, died on August 2, 1822. He

8. Elizabeth Ann Roe, *Reflections on Frontier Life, 226.*

was buried in Spadra Buff, but in 1833. Sons and friends of Eddyville, disinterred his body and buried in it in the River View cemetery, next to his beloved daughter, Lorraine.

Even his death did not end the story of Matthew Lyon. Aleine Austin narrated what happened when Lyon's remains came to Eddyville. "Matthew Lyon departed this world as he had lived it—with flourish. Since the Indians had claimed they had preserved the body when they buried him more than ten years earlier, his admirers lifted the lid of the coffin to take one last parting look at him When the air touched his skin, the clear features of his face disintegrated, before their astonished eyes, and blew away to the four corners of the earth".[9] Perhaps this macabre scene was symbolic of the way Matthew Lyons' influence swept over the American nation.

J. Fairfax McLaughlin, in an early biography of Lyon (1900), wrote a fitting summary of the legacy Lyon left America. "Matthew Lyon . . . lamented by the whole American people; a man of action and deeds which left their imprint on his times; a patriot in every fiber, whose vote made a President; a pioneer along whose pathway Romance walked side by side with history, a hero whose memory is cherished in Kentucky and Vermont, among the foremost and bravest of their sons."[10]

In a remarkable way, Matthew Lyon's life from a young boy in Ireland escaping the tyranny of an occupying force to his initial journey in America as an indentured servant to his later role as a fighter for freedom in his new country to his later years fighting to free slaves, serves to illustrate his lifelong role as a defender of freedom.

Resisting tyranny in any form was the central theme of his life.

9. Austin, 194
10. McLaughlin, 474.

7. Letter to America

WHILE MATTHEW LYON OBVIOUSLY could not know personally those of us living in Twenty-First Century America, nor could he have envisioned what this country might have become, his life and words defending freedom still have meaning, a bridge between the centuries, a warning if you will of how to resist tyranny in our time and keep the Republic free. Based on his life and words, this is what he might have written to us who are living in the dawning decades of this century, perhaps with more need to resist tyranny and seek liberty than ever. This is an imaginative account of what he might say to use if we received a letter from him from the past to our present times. Hopefully, our ancestor will forgive us from taking such license, but we believe he would not have been quiet these days any more than he was in times past.

Fellow Citizens:

I realize I am but an immigrant from Ireland brought here on a ship as an indentured servant, not knowing anyone and having been sold to a wealthy businessman to work off my indebtedness. It was very difficult leaving my poor Irish mother as she was sleeping and going to the ship to sail to the new world. I am not sure where I got the courage to do so. I only knew there was little future for me in my country of birth. My father, a patriot and rebel against British tyranny, was dead, and though I learned the printing trade,

I was still a youth in his teens coming to a new world with only the hope of starting a better life. Your country held out this hope to me and though I was sometimes called names and mistrusted because of my national origins, I worked hard to make a way because this was, after all, the land of freedom. I certainly hope by now you have learned to value your immigrants, for in my day they were the lifeblood of the republic. They, like me, may be the best resources for your future.

I remember once having an argument with a friend of mine who suggested that as a descendant of those who arrived on the Mayflower he was the true citizen, but he failed to note that others were already on this land, to welcome him as an immigrant and perhaps they also came to this new land from another. So, in a real way, we are all immigrants to this country we love because it took us in. I do not claim to be much of a religious man; in fact, my friend Ethan Allen and I used to talk about how pious people sometimes did more harm than atheists, but I do know one thing my mother told me and which I believe is at the heart of the Christian religion: love others as you wish to be loved. That is why I believe how you treat immigrants is how you will be judged, if not in the next life then in this one.

I was saddened to find, later in my life in America that in 1798 the Congress passed the Alien and Sedition Acts, part of which was directed toward limiting immigration into your country. That act added to the residency requirement so that the requirement for citizenship was increased from five to fourteen years and to make matters more ominous, it established a federal registry of all aliens, thus centralizing power at the federal level. The Alien Friends Act then gave the president power to deport aliens he suspected of being dangerous, but only in times of war. This act was not invoked. I surely must hope that by the time you read this letter your policies toward immigrants to your land will be more civilized.

I have no idea where you find the situation in your country now. We did our best to resist tyranny in our time, whether from an outside country like Britain, or the Federalists who tried to take away the freedom we fought to obtain by restricting voting. I bet there are still other countries trying to interfere in your nation and I don't doubt that there are some in your midst who are tyrants and want you to be their loyal servants. Resist their temptations, whether they claim they are only protecting you from outsiders or taking away your freedoms in the name of security. Watch what they do, not just what they say.

I went to jail for speaking against President John Adams. He wanted to stifle free speech, especially any words directed against him. You were created to think and act for yourselves, not be puppets for some supposedly small, elite group who pride themselves on putting you down and themselves up. Beware of any leader who has never had to work a day in his life but inherited his wealth from a father. Beware of any leader who tells lies rather than truths, who disguises his real intentions by beguiling you with fancy words and promises.

I also want to caution you about segregating your country into those who are rich and powerful and those who are not. Remember, I was someone who built his life out of the sweat of his own brow. I came with nothing and worked hard to learn a trade. And from such humble beginnings I started two new towns in my lifetime, each one in a wilderness. I did not inherit a title or money. I did not graduate from the best schools, such as Yale or

Harvard. Mine was the school of life and from this I learned how to succeed.

Here's the real rub: When those who are rich and powerful in business take over government, they try to impose on it what they learned in their private worlds—and it just doesn't work the same. I should know; I went from being a laborer and small businessman to running a mill and factory. When I went to Congress, I thought I could transfer the skills I learned in running a business to that of running a government. Serving the people is not the same as serving the bottom line. The best skill is how you deal with people, both those you serve and those you work alongside. You can't fire your constituents nor the president, though there were many times I wish I could have fired John Adams. He tried to tell me and others what to think and how to vote and when we turned on him, he sought to destroy us. He didn't succeed. I, and many others like me, serve the people, not the president. When I took the oath of office to defend the Constitution, I didn't think I would have to do so against the president's desire to bypass it by leading the way in passing laws to control our criticisms of him. John Adams might have appeared strong, but he was thin- skinned and egotistical, thinking he was more important than the people and Constitution he had pledged to support. Leaders become tyrants when they try to get by force what they can't get by persuasion.

In my time, it was the great desire of people to be free; that drove them to serve the country in many ways, whether in the military, business or government. We debated and argued and spoke to one another in town meetings and wherever we could. The New England town meeting was the heart of democracy where a person had to argue his case with his neighbors and with those charged with representing him. It was personal and up close. And those we elected could not hide from the people either. I don't know what you are doing these days, but I know in my time we talked openly and so did our representatives. Sometimes, I know, it could get rough. I got into a real fight on the floor of the house in the congressional hall in Philadelphia. Those days, it mattered what you believed, I suppose, though thinking back I wish I had handled it better. Maybe that's why when I first came to Congress from Vermont, they warned about the "mad Lyon" coming to town.

So, what would I advise you fellow citizens of the future?

First, beware of those who in the name of liberty try to take away your own. They start with the First Amendment and seek to dismantle it with new laws or seizing more power for themselves all the while telling you otherwise.

I don't like big government either, but I worry about those who seek to do away with the most important functions of the state to promote their own interests. They go after Congress and the courts first, especially trying to pass new laws to restrict the rights of people to speak and assemble freely. They'll try to use the courts to serve their own needs, not those of the citizens. And then they'll turn their full attention on negating free speech, whether of private citizens or newspapers. I should know—I was a newspaper publisher. They didn't like what I wrote and used some of it to try me for telling what I saw as the truth about our president, that he was acting like a high and mighty king with everyone else his loyal subjects. We had partisan newspapers in my day, some favoring the Federalists and John Adams and others the Republicans and Thomas Jefferson. One of my friends, Benjamin Franklin Bache of

Philadelphia, was indicted for libel. One night a mob even tried to destroy his home. Bache was fearless in his criticisms of the Federalists and John Adams in his newspaper, The Aurora.

In reflecting on my own life as an immigrant and a defender of liberty, I've been thinking a great deal about what I would advise future generations of Americans. I remember the story told about my friend, Ben Franklin, when someone reportedly asked him after the Constitution was drafted: "Well, Doctor, what have we got—a republic or a monarchy?"Dr. Franklin replied: "A republic, if you can keep it."I've spoken with Ben many times afterwards, especially since I sent my son to learn the printing trade with him in Philadelphia. We talked about our republic and how it was going. From these conversations and my own life, here are some words of advice on how to keep your republic, if in fact, there still is one.

I know my friend Thomas Jefferson is credited with writing that "eternal vigilance is the price of liberty," but I think otherwise. In a July 10, 1790 speech in Dublin, Ireland, John Philpot Curren, a politician, said: "The condition upon which God hath given liberty to man is eternal vigilance."

What do you who live in America today need to be vigilant of to protect your liberty?

First and foremost, protect and defend your First Amendment. It is the very source of your freedom, and anyone who seeks to diminish the protections therein is not a patriot. So, let me remind you of those precious rights we defined in 1789: "Congress shall make no law respecting an establishment of religion, or prohibiting the free exercise thereof; or abridging the freedom of speech or of the press; or the right of the people peaceably to assemble, and to petition the government for a redress of grievances."You can spot tyranny when those who can limit freedom (and, please remember this power is reserved to the congress, not the president) by discriminating against any religion or seeking to bar it from the country, when it tries to limit the freedom to speak or that of the press, or prohibit people from gathering to protest governmental actions. Jefferson also warned: "When the speech condemns a free press, you are listening to a tyrant."

Second, beware when too much power is invested in too few people, whether in business or politics, but most especially when each is joined together in an unholy alliance. Too much power in too few hands can lead to tyranny and often to its abuse. As I understand the Founders, some, like Federalists, wanted more power in a national government while Republicans, my party, wanted a weaker central government with more power given over to states. I came to believe that the best decisions are ones where local citizens retain the power, but that it is shared with other levels of government. For example, I have served in all three governmental levels—local, state, and federal—but government seems to work best when these levels work in harmony with one another, and especially in concert with the citizens. Of course, in my day, I knew my citizens and their needs. I am not sure whether this still holds in your time.

Third, beware of foreign alliances. How well I remember the words warning us against foreign alliances by our departing President George Washington. He didn't say we shouldn't have them; he just cautioned against finding our country taken over by another, as he might well have thought after fighting the British. Of course, in that same address, he warned against the divisions caused by political parties. I confess I belonged to one of *the new ones and the frictions between mine and that of John Adams were terribly difficult and, I must admit, harmful to working together to solve national problems. If your parties do nothing but fight among themselves and not for the people, throw them out of office. Politics was meant to be a public service, not a permanent job.*

Fourth, protect and defend your republic, whether from without or within. I believe the worst threats come from within, those who would subvert the values we uphold, as Jefferson wrote, of life, liberty and the pursuit of happiness.

In two simple words, this would be my best guidance for keeping your Republic healthy:Resist tyranny.

Just as I remember school teachers giving us lists to memorize, I would ask that you write down the list below and read it from to time in your times to remember what is important:

Take being a citizen seriously.

Organize for good causes.

Work for leaders who support all the people, not just a few of them.

Vote as if your life depended on it, because it does.

Speak out against oppression of all kinds, whether of the heart or mind.

Keep leaders under watch; the best form of leadership in a democracy is that of citizen patriots, not permanent office holders.

Seek truth.

Challenge lies.

And when the government seems to be corrupt, it is your patriotic duty to change those who lead it.

This my sincere prayer for you.

M. LYON

Suggested Reading

Life of Matthew Lyon

Austin, Aleine, *Matthew Lyon, "New Man" of the Democratic Revolution*, 1749-1822. University Park: Pennsylvania State University, 1981.

McLaughlin, Fairfax, *Matthew Lyon, The Hampden of Congress, A Biography*. Originally published, 1900. New York: Forgotten Books, 2012.

Elizabeth Ann Lyon Roe, *Recollections of Frontier Life. (1885)*. Forgotten Books, 2012.

———. *Aunt Lemma* or *Early Life on the Frontier*. 1885

Odell Walker, *Profiles of the Past. 1995_*

In Lyon County, Saturday was Town Day. Lyon County Historical Society. 2002.

Alien and Sedition Acts

Halperin, Terri Dianne, *The Alien and Sedition Acts of 1798,* Baltimore, Md., Johns Hopkins Press, 2016.

Miller, John C., *Crisis in Freedom: The Alien and Sedition Acts,* Boston, 1951.

Smith, James Morton, *Freedom Fetters. The Alien and Sedition Acts and American Liberties,* Ithaca, New York: Cornell University Press ,1966 [1956].

Free Speech and Freedom of the Press

Rosenfeld, Richard N., *American Aurora: A Democratic-Republican Returns,* New York: St. Martin's Press 1997.

Slack, Charles, *Liberty's First Crisis, Adams, Jefferson and the Misfits Who Saved Free Speech,* New York: Atlantic Monthly Press. 2015.

Snyder, Timothy, *On Tyranny: Twenty Lessons From the Twentieth Century.* New York: Tim Duggan Books, 2017.

Appendix

First Amendment to the
U.S. Constitution 1791

"Congress shall make no law respecting an establishment of religion, or prohibiting the free exercise thereof; or abridging the freedom of speech, or of the press; or the right of the people peaceably to assemble, and to petition the Government for a redress of grievances."

Section 2, Alien and
Sedition Acts of 1798

"And be it further enacted, That if any person shall write, print, utter or publish, or shall cause or procure to be written, printed, uttered or published, or shall knowingly and willingly assist or aid in writing, printing, uttering or publishing any false, scandalous and malicious writing or writings against the government of the United States, or either House of the Congress of the United States, or the President of the United States, with intent to defame the said government, or either House of the said Congress, or the said President, or to bring them, or either of them, into contempt or disrepute; or to excite against them, or either or any of them, the hatred of the good people of the United States, or to stir up seditions within the United States; or to excite any unlawful combinations therein, for opposing or resisting any law of the United States, or any act of the President of the United States, done in pursuance of any such law, or of the powers in him vested by the Constitution of the United States; or to resist, oppose, or defeat any such law or act, or to aid, encourage or abet any hostile designs of any foreign nation against the United States, their people or government, then such person, being thereof convicted before any court of the United States having jurisdiction thereof, shall be punished by a fine not exceeding two thousand dollars, and by imprisonment not exceeding two years."

Photo: Independence and Congress Halls, Philadelphia, Pennsylvania. Congress Hall is where Matthew Lyon served as a Vermont Congressman

About the Authors

John C. Morgan teaches philosophy and ethics at Albright College's Division of Professional Studies where he also holds his undergraduate degree in sociology. He also has two other master's degrees in philosophy and a doctorate. He is a newspaper and television columnist and author of eight books and many articles and poems. His latest book is *A Teacher, His Students and the Great Questions of Life*. He lives outside Philadelphia with his wife, a social worker. He has three children and two grandchildren.

Richard Lyon Morgan is a retired counselor and historian and presently an author. He was named for Rev. Richard Lyon of Camden, New Jersey. He earned five degrees, including a major in history from Davidson College, and a Ph.D. He is the author of 17 books which include *Remembering Your Story, General Daniel Morgan Reconsidered* and *Founded on the Rock: A History of Quaker Meadows Presbyterian Church* (Founded, 1775). He lives outside Pittsburgh. He has four children and ten grandchildren.

"This book makes for fine reading, not just for its story value. *Resisting Tyranny* also gives an insight into the dynamic of how tyranny can thrive, not just in Lyon's time, but our own. It speaks to the crucial importance of protecting our rights to free speech and a press."

—**Don Wendorf,** Retired Psychologist and Musician

"At a time when an U.S. President and his sycophants, and even religious advisors, are accusing the media of inventing' 'fake news,' this brief book inspires us to remind us of our priceless constitutional rights. This Irish-American and friend of Ethan Allen and the Green Mountain boys never feared to champion democracy against the pretensions and powers in both State and Church."

—**Dwyn Mounger,** Historian, American History

"The sheer genius of this book is found in the way of not only putting the average person in touch with this period of history, but to make it lessons relevant for today. It warns against governments who steps into tyranny to insure they can do what they desire to do against the will of the people."

—**Will Randolph,** Director of Office on Aging,
United Methodist Church

"This is a good time for the Morgan's book *Resisting Tyranny* to appear, as we live with Faulkner's declaration, 'The past is no dead, it's not even past.' Matthew Lyon's story needs to be revisited, as some of the challenges to democracy Lyon faced, we confront in our time. In a real sense Lyon's opposition to the then President John Adams Sedition Acts of 1798 is a mirror of what we face today in places of power. We need to heed Lyon's letter to future citizens take being a citizen seriously, 'to organize for good causes,' 'to seek truth,' and 'challenge lies,' if we are to preserve and extend our freedom. If not, the words of George Santayana may well come true, 'Those who cannot remember the past are condemned to repeat it.' This is a well written book without a dry word in it."

—**Jane M. Thibault,** Retired Gerontologist

"Penning a letter to the present generation in which they would imagine to be the words of their Irish ancestor, who rose to the level of statesman from the ranks of servanthood the Morgans' write, 'Protect and defend your republic, whether from within or without . . . the worse treats come from those who subvert the values we uphold.' I would highly recommend this book to any who seek to preserve the lessons of history, both for the betterment of themselves and the current generation, and those whose responsibility it will be to ensure the lives and liberties of all."

—**Daniel C. Potts,** Founder and President Cognitive Dynamics Foundation

"As an American History major, I certainly remember reading about the 1798 Alien and Sedition Acts, but I don't recall reading about Matthew Lyon, the first American tried, fined, and imprisoned under these very acts for speaking out against the then President John Adams. Matthew Lyon's life was dedicated to securing these ideals for himself, and for others, and in so doing, he became our country's first martyr for freedom of speech and the press. . ."

—**Lynda Everman,** Convener, Clergy Against Alzheimer's Network.

"Matthew Lyon is an oft overlook personage who played an important role in the founding and shaping of the nation. *Resist Tyranny*, written by two of Lyon's descendants is a brief but informative book that gives insight into this colorful character, whose spirit was filled with the proverbial Celtic fire. The Morgan brothers have done a fine job of introducing this lively and evocative patriot to a broad audience. It is fascinating and reader friendly."

—**David M. Seymour,** Pastor, Evangelical Lutheran Church in America

"By his industry and skill Matthew Lyon caved out an empire in both Vermont and Kentucky. Both John Adams and Matthew Lyon began their terms at the same time. For the next four years political sparks between Lyon and Adams flowed like fireworks. When confronted with Adams' attempt to stifle the tone of democracy written into the Constitution and the Bill of Rights, Lyon had a voice that could not be stilled. Matthew Lyon is almost a forgotten patriot and has been passed over by history. This effort to resurrect Life's life and political influence for our time is much needed."

—**Odell Walker,** Lyon County Historian and President of
the Lyon County Historical Society

"Matthew Lyon's sense of adventure brought him to America at an early age. Once here, his strong work ethic and flair for entrepreneurship served our fledgling country well. His legendary, outspoken patriotism and service to country will surely inspire the reader!"

—**Sally Whittington,** Lyon County Historical Society

"What better timing for the publication of this book. Our country is divided because of disagreements with the policies regarding immigrants. We now have freedom of speech to criticize the president and the administration. It is an appropriate time to be reminded that Matthew Lyon fought for this right."

—**Lorraine Brown IPP,** Fair Haven Vermont
Historical Society

"By bringing the life of Matthew Lyon to our attention, the Morgan brothers show us how easily the freedoms we enjoy can be restricted and urge us to be alert to the possibility of emergent tyranny in our own time. Although Lyon was engaged in public service more than 200 years ago, his determination to assert his (and now our) right to criticize the leaders of this democratic republic makes his story entirely relevant today. Everyone concerned about freedom of expression and the state of our union should read this succinct and highly interesting account of a remarkable defender of liberty."

—**Josiah Benjamin Richards,** Author/compiler of *God of Our Fathers: Advice and Prayers of Our Nation's Founders*

Author Index

Subject Index

www.ingramcontent.com/pod-product-compliance
Lightning Source LLC
LaVergne TN
LVHW021622080426
835510LV00019B/2715